ROCKSTAR

Magnify Your Greatness in Times of Change

FOR WOMEN LEADERS

SARAH McVANEL

PUBLISHING

Sharon –
keep your
passionate
journey
to truly
"see" people.
Sarah

ISBN 978-0-9951572-5-5 (Paperback)
ISBN 978-0-9951572-6-2 (e-Book)
ISBN 978-0-9951572-7-9 (Audiobook)

Printed in Canada

Edited by: Catherine Leek of Green Onion Publishing
Cover and Interior Design and Layout by:
Kim Monteforte Book Design & Self-Publishing Services
Original Cover Design Concept by:
Azadeh Yaraghi of Gogo Telugo Creatives

Contents

How Do I Keep My Rockstars?

Okay, I'm just going to say it. Women are the rock to so many.

This statement is not meant to disparage anyone. All of us, no matter our gender, are the rock to someone – many someones, in fact.

This book is a part of the *ROCKSTAR: Magnify Your Greatness in Times of Change* series. Women are still looking for ways to support each other and, as a person who identifies as she/her, I am honored to be part of the narrative through the writing here.

> When I use the terms female or women, I am referring to those who identify as she/her. Many of the qualities and attributes, as well as the tips here, are applicable to all genders. For the purposes of this mini-book, research that is based on those who identify as she/her is referenced and used as the foundation for the thought leadership presented here. Just as I would welcome the request of other industries to have their own *ROCKSTAR* version, other genders are welcome to suggest this and provide feedback via my website at greatnessmagnified.com/contact.

Slow Progress Is Still Progress

The quest for equality, satisfaction and meaning for women's contributions continues. Although we are making inroads in this regard at work, according to McKinsey,[1] those who identify as she/her are still underrepresented, particularly women of color. There continues to be disparity in pay[2] and it still takes longer for women to advance professionally.[3] When promoted, interestingly, women are more likely than men to be appointed to top jobs when the organization is in crisis. This "glass cliff"[4] makes it

For the content of references noted in this chapter, please see: greatnessmagnified.com/rockstar.

harder for those who identify as she/her to showcase their abilities as it is more challenging to be successful.[5]

Head down and plow through is what the Women of Influence[6] found was one of the pitfalls of women's advancement. Coming out of the pandemic, those who identify as she/her shouldered a great economic toll[7] as well as burnout.[8] All of these factors point to key reasons why *ROCKSTAR for Women Leaders* is relevant now.

1. Women need to adapt, change and flex, yet it can take a toll.
2. Women are making key decisions about the future of career and lifestyle.
3. Women may be underrepresented, however they're a powerful force in workplace trends.

Added to these arguments is the data that those who identify as she/her still bear greater non-work responsibilities.[9] [10] In Canada, over **75%** of women are engaged in paid work outside the home,[11] although they are paid less than their male counterparts.[12] Women are making inroads, in increasing numbers, into middle management positions, including top-job CEO roles, yet we are still grossly underrepresented on Boards of Directors in the US.[13]

Never doubt you earned where you are and own it. It didn't come by chance or luck. You earned it with hard work and incredible skills.

Erin, General Manager

The data doesn't lie. There is more to be done.

In the spirit of empowerment, this book is about **what we can do every day to move the needle forward** for ourselves, our colleagues, those who report to us and the generations of those who identify as she/her who will follow. This is not to say it should all fall on us to create change; *ROCKSTAR for Women Leaders* is about the practical strategies that make us effective, successful and productive *while* we are on the journey to greater equality.

An Unexpected Opportunity

People are forever changed post-pandemic. Individuals of all genders are expecting greater flexibility, psychological safety, fair compensation and equality. This isn't down to the pandemic alone though.

The requests of the past are the trends of today.

At the time of writing, we happen to be in an employee-driven marketplace with a talent shortage, enabling employees and middle managers to "vote with their feet," right out the door of their current employer, and even their industry if there is a better option elsewhere.

The biggest global healthcare crisis of our lifetime has resulted in the unintended and unanticipated consequences of what Dr. James Hollis[14] called, "a meeting with ourselves." People of all genders are considering these options, among other big questions.

- How do I feel about my employer, my industry, my colleagues?
- How does work fit into the bigger picture of my life?
- How can I ensure work doesn't negatively impact my physical health, mental health, lifestyle and relationships?

In other words, not only is there the opportunity for change in our employee-driven workforce, **there is now an increased comfort with job and career change** as well.

Change in our external environment and change in our inner landscape = greater expectation for change within our workplaces too.

Inner Knowing + External Environment = Opportunity for Change

We have a window of time to capitalize on the opportunity that those who identify as she/her have wanted and needed in the world of work. We want to continue to be the ROCK, and yet it can feel like a boulder pressing down on our shoulders.[15] We want to get STAR results, for ourselves and our workplaces. (More on how this builds into an acronym soon.) We're positioned, at this time in history, to gain momentum; the data is illustrating how burdened we are, so let's ground ourselves in how to practically make the most of our current opportunity for change at work.

We have decided the place we spend most of our waking hours needs to be scrumptious, energizing, an empowering part of our identities. We deserve nothing less.

How to ROCK as a Leader

Whether we are exactly where we planned to be, being the rock to those around us will always be expected and, frankly, that makes us feel more satisfied, confident and passionate. Being able to **support others and not deplete ourselves – human giver syndrome[16] – is a key opportunity for**

those who identify as she/her to personally thrive through change as well as mentor and manage others through it.

While we're at it, let's deal with perfectionism.[17] Unrealistic expectations of ourselves weigh us down with guilt and unvalidated beliefs that we're not doing or being enough. **Change resilience requires us to become more acquainted with a failure-friendly mindset.** Being aware of and shaking off unhelpful social norms, family of origin experiences and deeply entrenched expectations is part of the personal *and* professional journey for all of us.[18] As so many women shared in a previous book, *Flip Side of Failing*, the more we fail, ironically, the more successes we experience. We may know this fact but how comfortable are we with this truth, particularly when others are depending on us.

Together, let's lean into how to ROCK – Recognize, Organize, Communicate with Kindness – in order to get STAR – Satisfaction, Teamwork, Achievement, and Retention – results for ourselves and others. We actually do this very well.[19] How can we be even more intentional about this? Now that is a delicious opportunity.

Don't second guess yourself and your capabilities. Just go for it. It's either going to be a good time or a good story!

Toral, Leadership Coach

Within the pages of this book, practical strategies, validated evidence and advice from fellow women enable the building and deepening of a practical toolkit for change readiness and, ultimately, greater success and satisfaction at work.

Outside these pages, you'll find resources and the content for the references noted in each chapter. Just scan this QR Code.

Although it's written with those who identify as she/her in mind, the insights here can benefit us all. The call to action and examples may be gender specific, however the desire for us all to do meaningful work, nurture the next generation of leaders, have satisfying work and home lives, feel less chaos from change at work and retain great people is shared by all.

Let's jump in rockstars. We have much to do and even more to celebrate!

CHAPTER 1

Change as Opportunity

Imagine with me for a moment.

It's Sunday night. As you turn your mind to the week ahead, you notice how you're not dreading Monday morning. Yes, there is a lot on your plate, however you feel a sense of excitement about what lays ahead.

You reflect on how much more enjoyable it has been to recognize people and how you see it happening spontaneously in the team. It wasn't long ago you would dread team meetings and conversations with vocally negative people, however your approach to recognize first and respond second has built trust and improved communication exponentially.

You realize that you don't feel as weighed down, with all the responsibility to "fix things" resting only on you. It feels good to see so many on your team suggesting and making improvements, knowing that progress matters more than perfection. There is no blame.

You have been told multiple times recently how much other departments like working with your team, and customers are satisfied. It seems everyone feels more connected to their purpose.

You know you have a great future here with good gender representation in key roles. You have opportunities to stretch and grow, your voice is heard and you are respected. You know that your contributions would be missed if you left. So you stay. And it feels good given how much career change you're seeing in your peer group, scrambling to find the place they belong.

As you go into the week, you feel empowered to mentor and support people of all genders to feel successful, understood and psychologically safe. You are happy, right where you are.

Now, ask yourself, on a scale of 10 to 1, with 10 being "absolutely true" and 1 the opposite of that, to what extent is this an accurate description of your current reality?

Does this seem like a work of fiction, a fairy tale? Although people rarely describe their employment this way, I have worked with leaders, including those in very senior roles, who identify with much of this. Perhaps more to the point, don't we all deserve to work toward this?

Is it helping our quest for gender equality, work-life balance, psychologically safe work and overall career satisfaction to write this off as "impossible"?

The Job – Then and Now

For as long as I can remember, my dad, well intentioned as he was, tried to help me understand that with work you must grin and bear it, develop a thick skin, put up with bullies, ignore mean bosses, expect disrespectful customers, manage unreasonable hours and tolerate overwhelming workloads. That was, he believed, part of the deal to get a paycheck.

It *was* his reality. Does it have to be?

> The glass ceiling is real, so do not sell your soul for work. Take from your career what you need for yourself and those important in your life.
>
> Andrea, Healthcare Leader

Today, employees of all genders are saying no way! Our talent shortage is paving the way for the potential to have a more respectful, inclusive, fairly compensated and balanced workplace that we all deserve – and have always wanted. Even as the pendulum swings, and it inevitably does, our workforce's expectations have forever changed. Employees and managers are calling more of the shots, and what they're calling for is better for everyone.

The average number of jobs a person holds in their lifetime now sits at thirteen (give or take depending on the study).[20] Not only are people switching jobs, they are taking the leap to other organizations, industries and sectors. **Turnover is here to stay. Many will retrain to grasp the future they want.**

There are more career choices than ever before. New roles and industries. Access to education. A global market to explore given the rise in remote work. A thriving gig economy. And an overall willingness to ask for what we want and need. This is a beautiful opportunity for those who identify as she/her given the inequities that still exist.

They're also shopping for leaders.

- Do I want to work for someone who is flexible and values work-life balance?
- Do I need a mentor who will support me to stretch and grow?
- Do I need someone who will hold me accountable and challenge me to surpass my limits?

Although there are unique factors that drive someone to value, say, flexibility over mentorship, the root question is: Does your leadership approach fit the needs of today?

Let's take this reflection one step deeper: **Would you work for yourself?**

For years Organizational/Industrial Psychologists have tried to identify and define the most important leadership competencies and, despite their brilliant brains, there isn't one set we can all agree on. Maybe this makes sense. Is there one type of leader that works for everyone? Is there one leadership benchmark to indicate that you officially possess all the leadership competencies in exactly the right amounts? Almost seems like an exercise in futility, doesn't it?

Despite the logic, how often do you ask yourself, "Am I doing a good job as a leader?" A great question if it's a healthy self-evaluation in the context of your current reality. More often, I find rockstar leaders who identify as she/her come from a place of "I am not enough." It's a cataloging of all the ways they are lacking.

Remember, you have no benchmark to evaluate yourself against. Maybe the question needs to be, "Am I doing the best I can?" In other words, do you continually work *toward* being the type of leader people want to work with?

This is what being the rock to your staff, peers and customers is all about. You do your best for the many who depend on you while also juggling the competing demands on your shoulders.

Great leaders deal with disrespect, dispel rumors, handle ineffective processes, ditch burnout-inducing demands, determine priorities, delineate responsibilities and dish out appreciation abundantly. This isn't to say you need to be superhuman. This is to say that great leaders are so human that they try to ensure that humanity is ever present at work.

What you do when the chips are down is what people remember. Your visibility, communication, empathy, appreciation and decision-making prowess are essential – and under a microscope in times of change and strain. This can be a time when we doubt ourselves most; it can also be what defines us.

When you stand in your power, you stand to empower.

ROCKSTAR for Women Leaders is designed to help you stay focused on what matters most during stressful, distracted and overwhelming times so you can be that rock to others. Your greatness will magnify the greatness of those around you.

Your Call to Lead

Leaders, you have never been more needed than you are now. Even if you never jump in to help out – which, of course, is a great way to show you are right alongside your direct reports – your ability to address unnecessary roadblocks, detect potential turnover and ensure individuals feel valued, heard and appreciated cannot be underestimated. How do you do that when there is too much to do, decisions to make with partial information and you are running on too little sleep yourself?

We are at risk of doing to versus with. Telling versus talking. Coping versus comforting.

Here's what I fear, and often see. We take the need to centralize decision-making one step too far. It all falls on leaders to plan and make choices, and staff (and middle managers) are dispersed to go and do. Then, when things are not working, you think it's all down to you – you must have all the answers, ensure everyone is working hard enough, dictate versus engage – and staff feel disconnected from you. The communication is too one-way, the fixes are stalled and the "us and them" gap widens.

You may work in a system that reinforces these mismatches. It can be tough. Sometimes it requires some self-leadership to navigate.

The reality is you may feel uncomfortable saying "I don't know" or even "no." Ironically, it is being *with* people when you learn what's really going on and what deeper issues are at play. Respect and trust are foundational to honesty. **People won't tell you what you don't want to hear unless they believe their voice matters.**

We know people aren't disposable. Your people aren't Chinet®. They are Royal Dalton, limited-edition, gold-plated, heirloom-quality human beings. They only ever *appreciate* in value if you *appreciate* them.

And we wonder why engagement is so low.

Your workforce is savvier than ever. Gallop found that it takes a 20% pay raise to entice someone away from a manager who engages them.[21] They're watching how you act, if they like it and how much they matter to you.

People are intuitive. When we treat people like they're just a number (title, role, job classification), it makes it easier for them to leave. Why would they stay? You care though.

In a recent study, staff who rated their leader in the top 10% for recognition were more engaged – 68th percentile versus the 27th percentile, where leaders regarded people as a number or disposable.[22] They will stay because you treat them like they matter, because you believe they do. No matter your tenure, role or support, what is within your control is that you can always treat people like they matter. And, you cannot afford not to. Not anymore.

> *Don't take criticism from those you wouldn't go to for advice.*
>
> Deb, Organizational Behavior Expert

Engagement Is Table Stakes

Besides needing every single person, we also need their ideas, solutions and strengths to enable innovation, hope and creativity to get through and come out the other side better off. Your talent won't bring it to bear if your team doesn't feel what they bring is valued.

On-the-job retired or on-the-job inspired.

You can turn up engagement now, through ROCK leadership behaviors we'll explore in the coming chapters, and watch it grow exponentially. As engagement swells, you'll see STAR outcomes as a result.

I have yet to meet a staff member, leader or team where feeling appreciated (Recognition), doing work efficiently (Organized), understanding what's going on (Communication), and being treated with respect (Kindness) wasn't important. (More on these ROCK behaviors in Chapter 2.)

When one or more of these aspects aren't present, we don't get the best from people because they are *encumbered* and unable to give their best. When the pressure is on and uncertainty rises during change, we owe it to our teams to amp up awareness of what needs a course correction for what stands in the way of Satisfaction and performance (ideas about how to do this at the end of each ROCK chapter).

No Two Rocks Look the Same

In the pages that follow, I will deliver a practical leadership approach that will provide results during and after a crisis or change. In fact, you'll find it is foundational every day, and becomes non-negotiable as pressure rises.

Exactly how ROCK is implemented into your unique organization, leadership style and team is distinctive. That's a good thing. I invite you to continually ask yourself as you read this book:

- What works for me?
- What did X (think of a mentor or role model) do that worked so well?
- What did I do the last time that worked?

Tempted to save this to pass on to a fellow leader who identifies as she/her? If this stops you from marking up the book, e-mail us at books@greatnessmagnified.com with her name and address, and we'll send you a copy to gift to others on your behalf. Seriously, we will.

I will offer ideas, but **you are the expert in what works for you.** You know best what has worked (and not worked.) Be leery about "we've tried that" and consider, "what have we learned and can adapt." Build on that knowledge with what you read here.

To that end, you are welcome to mark up this book. Add asterisks, highlight ideas, cross out propositions that don't apply, make notes in the margins and scribble your action steps and juicy "aha" flashes on the inside covers. Talk about it at your meetings. Ask people to hold you accountable. Ask your trusted advisors what works for them.

Throughout the book, you will see this QR Code and scanning it will also get you to lots of great resources to aid you in being the ROCKSTAR leader you and your employees deserve. You will also find all the content for the references noted in each chapter.

Every one of you, regardless of industry, deserves to feel empowered, confident, competent, successful and healthy, so this book is a testament to you, rockstar. Let's dig in.

CHAPTER 2

ROCK Behaviors = STAR Outcomes

Do you ever feel like you're juggling too many balls – home, work, friends? Do you feel you need to take it on yourself, hesitate to ask for help, find yourself thinking "by the time I explain it to someone I might as well have done it myself."

Yep, I get it. No matter your circumstances, as a community of leaders who identify as she/her, we can redefine what supporting and inspiring others means and actually get better results for ourselves and others.

ROCK Leadership

When I ask leaders in coaching what their most effective leadership practices are, many struggle to honor their own effectiveness and put words to their greatest leadership assets. Maybe I work with a lot of humble folks, but the research on those who identify as she/her in leadership,[23] [24] the discomfort with conflict that coincides with women-dominated industries, such as the helping professions,[25] [26] [27] and the sheer consistency of this behavior tells me it's real. Even when we have the list of leadership competencies, there isn't always confidence that these are the right or most important behaviors or "best practices." If it's not considered a best and leading practice, well, is it even worth practicing?

Let me tell you what I've learned from working for 20+ years coaching and training leaders. There are four leadership behaviors that allow you to be the **ROCK** people need and desire, particularly in times of crisis and change.

1. Recognize
2. Organize
3. Communicate
4. Kindness

I can guess what you're thinking. I've heard this all before.

Bear with me. Are you 100% confident, beyond a shadow of a doubt, that you and all your leaders are practicing ROCK leadership behaviors right now? (Hey, we're not perfect! That said, you are not likely to reap the rewards in the long run.)

> *What I see as a huge opportunity for us lies in mentoring our female co-workers. There is a cost involved in not doing so.*
>
> Georgie, Manager

If practicing ROCK leadership behaviors during a challenging time or significant change brings out the best in staff, imagine the impact if it formed the foundation of everyday behavior of leaders and staff. Would you still be worrying about engagement levels, concerned staff were run down or diligently filling openings vacated by unfulfilled former team members? **If you're a ROCK to your staff and teams, they will deliver STAR outcomes for you.**

Building Toward STAR Results

You know how on a clear night you can look up into the sky and see the cosmos full of stars? Have you ever wondered, "Hey, have I been missing seeing this all along?" Crisis, change and strain creates an opportunity to pause and, if we choose to accept the invitation, to reimagine "what is possible?" Given the fact there's already noise, chaos and stress, it's an opportunity to look up from our work world, get perspective and to come out the other side with improvements, efficiencies and deeper connections.

The more we look up from our laptops and intentionally connect with staff and tune into the pulse of our team and peers, the more we realize that the change is small in the grand scheme of things. However, the *people* in the midst of it are the important part. It's easy to miss the things that are in our environment all the time. Do you register the color of your front door every time you look at it or is it just part of the house?

It's the same with our people. They're always there. Our responsibility as "people leaders" is just part of the role, our tasks related to people are a constant. However, how we show up for and with people during significant and tough times are culture- and relationship-defining opportunities.

We need to amplify the people part of our role with concerted focus. With a mindset of "together," you may find you have a new take on the change too. These ROCK leadership practices are also a way to make you jazzed about your role too.

Momentum is a byproduct of movement. *Change* is movement; *movement* is energy; *energy* is empowerment; *empowerment* is potential.

When you put this time in context, you can see how these small but important leanings into ROCK leadership behaviors facilitate the big picture affairs that matter most in the short and long term.

Be proud of who you are! Keep your head up high and have a bounce to your step. Confidence is key!

Erica, Community Leader

- Satisfaction
- Teamwork
- Accomplishment
- Retention

Neuro-Linguistic Programming experts have shown that the brain that registers "anxiousness" can be reoriented to register that arousal as "excited."[28] You and those who depend on you can **shift from "we're nervous" to "we are excited" through ROCK leadership** and by continually focusing on the *result* and preferred future that change can create.

Let's not squander the opportunity to create your preferred future. Let's use change to supercharge, accelerate and amplify success. What a shift in thinking from the "change is hard" mantra we throw around like confetti, but without the fun!

Progress Not Perfection

Being the ROCK and aiming for STAR results is not about perfection, unwavering optimism and goal attainment. It's about showing up every day with a "doing the best we can" intention and a "we did the best we could yesterday" belief. It's the continual attention to Recognize, Organize, Communicate and be Kind and then noticing the signs of Satisfaction, Teamwork, Accomplishment and Retention so that you can do more of what works.

If you want your organization and teams to be better off during and following a change – to feel a sense of pride, to be more loyal and to be a stronger, intact team – then read on. The wisdom and simple strategies will not only serve you well today, they'll help you lead with humanity and resiliency every day. And the great news is that it aligns with the gifts of leaders who identify as she/her rather than trying to "fit in" to the historically male-dominated leadership structure.

Let's make this a comeback story. Those are the most interesting stories, aren't they? Ready to rewrite the future? Let's go.

 Use this QR Code to access lots of great resources to aid you in being the ROCKSTAR leader you and your employees deserve. You will also find all the content for the references noted in this chapter.

CHAPTER 3

Recognition

One thing you never hear in an exit interview is, "I was too appreciated." Even less likely, "I couldn't get anything done from the constant complimenting!"

Wouldn't that be something?

You're more likely to read scathing criticism on *Glassdoor* about the lack of appreciation – being treated like a number, poorly trained yet criticized for "poor performance," dealing with nasty colleagues, being overworked. You may also be surprised that even your best performers are saying "no thanks" to promotions, and the corporate ladder collects dust from all the leadership vacancies.

It may seem like bad news. It's not. Recognition is something you can amp up right now. Isn't it comforting to know that you have a manageable solution to keep great people, motivate them to do their best work and to become a magnet to attract other great people?

What Everyone Needs

Think about the last time you felt truly valued by a boss and peers. How did you show up to your work? What did you think about going back to work after time off? How do you think about that role to this day, compared to others where you felt less valued?

There is one thing that every employee and manager needs – regardless of gender, tenure, industry, age, title – to be valued and recognized. If everyone needs it, why is it also commonly identified as lacking by employees in engagement surveys?[29]

People may need it, yet there is a lot of hesitation. Leaders ask:

- How do I make sure it's sincere?
- Is it safe to do this in our sensitive workplace today?
- What if people think I'm playing favorites?
- How do I Recognize everyone rather than the same people over and over again?
- I used to express Recognition but it didn't work. How do I do it so it works?
- Do various generations want to receive Recognition differently?
- What if it's just not my style?

When I hear these very legitimate and vulnerable questions from well-meaning people, I provide this advice.

- Remember it's about *intention*; you will experience less negative fallout from doing something for the right reasons than holding back out of fear.
- **Consider recognition a muscle;** you build up confidence and ease through reps, trial and error, and perhaps some coaching along the way.

Recognition is often subjected to the negativity bias – we weigh the potential for a negative outcome as more important than that of the positive outcome. Not only are we more likely to have positive results rather than a negative fallout, we are better able to solve significant issues in Recognition-rich cultures – retention, satisfaction, collaboration, productivity – through the intrinsic motivation Recognition fuels.

I recall to this day a leader taking two minutes to send an email of praise for my contributions. She made my week and I was motivated to continue with challenging initiatives.

Dianne, Board Chair

We have *experienced* the benefits of being valued, heard and appreciated, so we need to remember our own lived experience as a way to sustain a Recognition intention as well as to orient us on how to Recognize. In fact, you can start there, with the golden rule – treat others the way you want to be treated. In this case, Recognize others the way you want to be Recognized. It's what you feel comfortable with after all. Over time, you can seek to follow the platinum rule – treat others the way *they* want to be treated.

What Organizations Need

Like most aspects of organizational life, when individuals get what they need from work – satisfaction, a sense of team, a feeling of achievement, a sense of meaning – they are better contributors. When people feel appreciated, valued and heard, they're more likely to offer great ideas, build deeper connections with colleagues, ask for help, collaborate in tasks and projects, show accountability for quality work and show their customers and colleagues they are valued too.

For example, when healthcare providers are told regularly by their colleagues, other departments and leaders what they're doing well, why their contribution mattered and specifically who appreciated them and for what, they're more satisfied, connected and likely to stay.[30] Think about that from the patient's point of view for a second. Two nurses are equally qualified and competent. Would you prefer to have the nurse who was appreciated or the one who hadn't heard any positive affirmations for their work lately? Do you think one might be more optimistic, less likely to feel burnt out and maybe even find it easier to show compassion?

Recognition is the single easiest way to boost engagement and insulate against day-to-day burnout, overwhelm and compassion fatigue. It's never too late to address these issues, too, by amping up Recognition.

Ideally, you help individuals stay resourceful, hopeful and energized by knowing their work matters and they are not simply a number. Change – internally planned or externally imposed – can deplete reserves. Build it back up through intentional Recognition. Better yet, make it the bedrock of your culture so that there is a stockpile of work well-being to draw upon.

Techniques for Recognizing Others

Okay, so now you're sold – maybe you already were! The next logical question is, "Is there a way that most people want to be Recognized? In the midst of time constraints, high levels of emotion and resource limitations, you will be glad to know that the most desired forms of Recognition are actually pretty simple, take virtually no time and require no budget. As a previous book, *Forever Recognize Others' Greatness*,[31] demonstrates, you have three go-tos.

1. Say thank you (95%)
2. Give specific acknowledgment (92%)
3. Write a thank-you note (88%)

Not only are they easy to do, they also address big issues that would take buckets of time, planning and budget to address through other means. When you look at a dataset of a quarter of a million data points, pulling out the 20 most satisfied teams with recognition and analyzing them compared to the 20 least satisfied, you'll find a huge statistically significant difference in:[32]

- Innovation and continuous improvement,
- Trust in the organization,
- Satisfaction with leaders,
- Intention to stay and
- Overall engagement.

To get through tough times – massive change, disruption, strain, chaos – and ride the aftershock, **people need to believe they matter.** As busy as you are personally in managing the turbulence, take comfort that Recognizing others is good for you too.

1. *You feel more in control.* If there is one thing you always have within your control, it's making your people feel valued and appreciated.
2. *Your mood and motivation improve.* When you engage in positive social interactions, like Recognition, it increases motivation, elevates mood and fuels a greater sense of connection with others. (There is some fascinating research on the connection between oxytocin and dopamine I've cited if you want to read more about this.[33])

> *We are just human.*
> *Be yourself, respect*
> *one another.*
>
> Nancy, Organization
> Development Professional

In other words, when you burn out, give up and lose hope, there's no faster way to fill yourself back up than watching someone's reaction when you acknowledge them. Imagine how well your teams could thrive by continual Recognition before, during and after a crisis or change?

If you already do this, and want to keep it fresh, check the online resources for my list of over 100 ways you can Recognize people quickly and easily even when you have no time.

TIPS WHAT WORKS

- Collect examples. If you don't already have it, create an e-mail address for folks to send in good news stories, brag about colleagues and rave about innovations on the team.
- Say thank you – *all the time.*
- Write thank-you notes, cards or use an app like SendOutCards to appreciate people in writing.
- Create visible public spaces for Recognition like kudos boards.
- Include Recognition stories on your website to excite customers and future staff.
- Make texts or e-mails more personal by incorporating video, voice recordings and pictures.
- Use social media to encourage the public to Recognize your staff (such as a campaign with a specific hashtag).
- Celebrate professional weeks.
- Leverage your internal communication system or try external systems like Kudoboard.com.
- Keep recognition fresh.

TIPS WHAT LIKELY DOESN'T WORK

- Make Recognition sound "corporate."
- Wait until a change is over to say thanks.
- Move onto the next change without celebrating wins and overcoming struggles.
- Recognize data only or feelings only.
- Acknowledge some staff and departments only. Use this opportunity to highlight unsung heroes behind the scenes.

For more information and insights into Recognition, including a special resource of 100+ ways to recognize staff, scan the QR Code. You will also find all the content for the references noted in this chapter.

CHAPTER 4

Organize

Never enough time. Too much to do. And so very, very busy.

Do you hear these things in reply to the question, "So, how is work going these days?"

Busy can be a badge of honor. "I'm clearly indispensable with so many people depending on me and so much I'm responsible for." It is a sign of the time.

The Post-Pandemic Organization

When anyone who *could* work from home was sent home, it demonstrated that much of the work done in offices *could* be done remotely. How organizations have shifted to meet the increased expectation of flexible work may be different. Many have found ways to make it viable.

Even if you have one person working remotely part or all of the time, then you've had to look at how work is Organized.[34] When you add to that the fact that most organizations' workforces, or at least part of them, must be at work to perform their job, then you add a layer of perceived "fairness" in how work gets distributed, communicated, accomplished and, hopefully, celebrated.

Now, you can see this as problematic. However, many of the tools in this chapter help you, no matter your industry or work structure, to be more efficient, feel more on top of your obligations and track expectations.

Work wasn't seamlessly Organized before, so anyone who resists the new complexity in ways of working needs a shift in focus. What was revealed that wasn't working before you now have the clarity to address. COVID revealed cracks in our existing processes, systems and structures.

Crisis is the perfect opportunity to address cracks in Organization and barriers to productivity and quality.

Setting Priorities

Teams and organizations are notorious for having too many priorities. Many thought leaders say that if you have more than three top priorities, you have too many.[35]

One of the benefits of a crisis is that it acts as a clearing house for priorities; only what's truly important makes the cut. A not-for-profit Executive Director listened to her overwhelmed middle managers a few months into COVID. She advocated to her Board of Directors to pause all project work on KPIs (key performance indicators). Crisis created the pause.

It also revealed that when they were reintroduced, there was a resurgence of being overwhelmed. The realization at that point was that a greater grasp of continuous improvement (CI) was needed. Some CI leadership development *alongside* the reinstatement of projects and an effort to assign tasks under a point person, while taking into account how many assignments were doled out to a few, were steps in the right direction.

As the old adage goes, "if it were easy, we'd already be doing it." **If it were easy to prioritize, you'd have that ranked list already.** Some tough conversations and new ways of planning may be needed over time. Being the rock to your team may be acknowledging priority overload and confusion about expectations.

We're in a state of crisis; we move at a frantic pace. Slowing down, however, actually allows us to speed up, to focus, prioritize and realize what is important.

Dana, Business Owner

You shouldn't need to wait until people, including you, are overwhelmed to take a step back to evaluate what's on the plate. Make-work tasks, people's pet projects and flavors of the month create distraction, confusion and lack of progress. However, few organizations are diligent about cutting versus adding initiatives.

Is there a comfort in those you lead and work with to have real conversations about whether a project is really needed and how much?

Busting the Multitasking Myth

Wouldn't it be great to get more done with the time we have? Oh, the appeal of multitasking.

I have some bad news though. **Research shows we can't multitask.**[36] **What we can do is "serial task."**

Serial tasking happens when you switch back and forth between tasks in rapid succession – such as answering an e-mail then taking a call and reading an incoming text. You don't do an efficient job of either and are more liable to make mistakes.[37] You know this from personal experience.

We *think* we are staying on top of things, however we are actually rail-roading our productivity, slashing our creativity and robbing ourselves of the opportunity to get more strategic work done through hyper focus on what is the highest priority. Instead, researchers suggest "monotasking," focusing on one task by minimizing potential interruptions for a period of time and ideally until the task is completed.

Pushing strategic work to our "off time" is not the solution; besides negatively impacting our health and wellbeing, this nasty habit means we may not be saying "no" enough, pushing back on unreasonable demands, and finding better systems for organizing how we work.

To be the rock to so many, step back and reflect. What have you learned doesn't work – when emotions run high, when the number of assigned tasks are unreasonable, when the duties clearly aren't a good fit? Ask yourself:

> *Be confidently and unapologetically you. Establish and maintain boundaries.*
>
> Yvonne, Healthcare Leader

- Is there a better assignment or timeline?
- Is this project necessary?
- Is this problem stemming from a deeper issue?
- Is this going to have long-term consequences, such as turnover from workload?

Reality Check

In a crisis or during a massive change, you and your team can't handle more. Maybe you can *never* handle more. You like to believe you can and you may feel you can't say no. You need to stretch yourself to pick the top three, put all our energy into those, measure progress and build a sustainability plan, before moving onto the next priorities.

Here are some guidelines.

* *Meetings:* If it can be communicated in a memo, don't have a meeting. If meetings are a way to get work done, put in a mechanism to track tasks and who's accountable instead.
* *Priorities:* Streamline priorities. Be ruthless with what makes it onto your top priorities during *and after* this time. One new thing comes on, take one off.
* *Reports:* Cut (or temporarily hold) possible make-work projects like reports. Who reads them, what do they need, what is the purpose, what structure could make it faster to do and shorter to create (and read). Some you can't change. Make the rest more efficient or cut them.

When done well, how you streamline and Organize your communication, needs, decision-making and priority setting in a crisis (or as if it were a crisis) can be a lesson in prioritizing "need to dos" from "nice to dos." Rather than seeing this advice about cutting things out, see it as auditioning priorities and tasks into your and your team's limited time.

Through conversation, including healthy debate, we can helpfully challenge if there is a better way to cut through "this is the way we've always done it."

Key Questions

Here are some questions you can reflect on and even engage others in a conversation about.

* If a crisis happened tomorrow, what meetings, communications and projects could be put on hold or canceled?
* Looking at that list, what will you pause to ensure there aren't negative implications to customers and culture?
* How can you free up essential people's time, including middle managers?
* What clarity is required so that people know what is expected of them?
* Do you have all the resources and skills needed on the team? If not, who has the transferable skills and can be redeployed to fill the gap?
* What communication systems are required to keep people in the know, feeling supported and productive?

By asking these types of questions, you can begin to **consider the four Ds of prioritization: Delegate, Defer, Diminish, Delete.**[38] The key component is balancing the removal of unnecessary aspects with the addition of necessary facets.

A "command and control" autocratic leadership style is not the natural style of leaders who identify as she/her.[39] We have other assets to draw from that can help. Decades of research out of Duke University has revealed women's model of "agency" as a leader includes competence, ambition, dominance, diligence, independence and self-assuredness. These attributes are key to being able to clearly, supportively and perseveringly move the conversation forward about what is possible versus what must be tolerated.

TIPS▶ *WHAT WORKS*

- Remove unnecessary projects and priorities.
- Streamline and shorten meetings.
- Introduce touch points and knowledge-exchange systems to keep communication and action on track.
- Trial efficiency tools and technology solutions (e.g., Slack, Trello, ThoughtExchange).
- If something is done more than once, put in a checklist, system or tool to reduce error or rework.
- Use internal cloud solutions or external (e.g., Google Drive) to house and share documents, presentations and spreadsheets.
- Have a simple naming system for documents and note revisions, such as history/date in the footer.
- Audit naming system and electronic filing system to ensure working as intended.
- Create main documents with links to additional resources on the cloud, intranet and internet.

TIPS▶ *WHAT LIKELY DOESN'T WORK*

- Leave it to people to figure out what is needed from them.
- Allow any non-priority work to remain (e.g., reports, projects).
- Ignore broken, inefficient processes because "there is no time" to fix it.

- Use meetings as accountability mechanisms to make sure tasks get done.
- Use your e-mail inbox as a document storage and sharing system.

For fabulous Organize information and insights, and all the content for the references noted in this chapter, be sure to scan the QR Code.

CHAPTER 5

Communicate

E-mail, voice mail, phone, text, WhatsApp, Voxer, Google Chat, Facebook Messenger, Instagram direct messaging, LinkedIn, MS Teams. Alert! Notification! Ping!

Streamlining Communication

It seems more than ever before there are an infinite number of ways that people can contact you. And as much as the previous chapter discussed how many systems for Organization can help manage your growing and competing priorities, we haven't said, "Okay, if that new technology is on the list, this outdated one is coming off."

How can you? One staff member prefers to contact you this way, another that way. As one human resources manager shared with me, the busier she gets, the more folks look for other ways to get hold of her for immediate answers. And app notifications alert you all day long as a friendly nudge to track your water or learn that other language. Before long, you're so inundated with communication you have no time to think let alone do!

It's what psychologists call "mental labor"[40] – when you spend time thinking about obligations even when you are doing something else, like thinking about work while at home and vice versa. It can be exacerbated by the litany of communication inputs and modalities. Even if you decide you won't give into the temptation of answering the e-mails flooding in on weekends, your brain might be there.

And if you find yourself working in a global context where you have contractors, colleagues and clients from other time zones, the situation is intensified. Good luck saying to them, "I know great client X you prefer for us to meet at 8am your time, however that's when I'm at my maximum REM cycle, so you call me in the middle of *your* night."

If there doesn't seem to be an appetite for truly eliminating communication inputs at work and there seems to be a new attention-grabbing communication distraction being added daily (okay maybe it's only monthly), the onus is on you to:

1. Decisively determine what modalities work best for home and eliminate others,
2. Challenge when new communication modalities are added at work, engage in a conversation about what other modes will be "retired" and
3. Reinforce respectfully what has been agreed upon.

I know what you're thinking. "Okay, Pollyanna, you haven't met my boss/kids/mom/condo association!" You are right. However, in an age where there will only ever be *more* modes of communication, for the sake of your productivity, well-being and integrity of your relationships, you must have a "less is more" mentality when it comes to communication.

You Matter to Me

People need to feel they matter to you (see Recognition). Brené Brown said, "Connection is the energy that exists when people feel seen, heard and valued." Are you truly connecting? Isn't communication designed to do that? Are you feeling fulfilled with how you are communicating with others – professionally and personally?

To rock as a leader, it will likely require some discipline to turn off the distractions, push back on the interfering modalities, and put up some boundaries in how often, where and why people can reach you.

True meaningful connection and productive exchanges fuel even deeper work relationships. When you choose to focus, listen deeply and engage in a feedback loop, you will not only make the person you are speaking with feel Recognized in that exchange, you also will be rewarded by learning about what is *really* going on, enabling you to make better decisions and you'll feel more Satisfied yourself.

My boss always makes time. When we're talking, she makes me feel like I'm the only one that matters. I try to be that way for my team too.

Sue, Human Resources Manager

By the way, e-mails are not the enemy. If you've been thinking, "So what do we do with my inbox of e-mails? I can't just delete them and talk to my staff all day!" Remember, your electronic communication also has the power to make people feel important too.

* Respond quickly.
* Include only the necessary people.
* Attach links to folders where content has been Organized versus attaching documents.
* Make subject lines helpful (e.g., FYI, Decision Required).
* Take tense electronic exchanges offline (in-person or virtual live meeting).
* Add a compliment to your standard sign-off, such as "Thanks for being reliably prompt."

See the connection to Recognize and Organize that we've already discussed? Maybe when people say "we don't communicate well" they also mean they want their needs met as much as they need the mechanics and amount of Communication to be improved.

Serve Versus Tell

When you question the "how," you also naturally question the substance of what you're communicating. Interestingly, when I coach leaders who feel overwhelmed by the demands on their time and barriers to feeling they are Communicating well, it's not long before they have an epiphany that to "get it done" has led to more telling to than engaging with.

Ultimately, Communication is a reflection of your culture. What insights would a new staff member or leader glean from simply observing Communication (written and verbal)? In fact, why not ask one? It's hard to see the label from inside the jar.

It helps to flip your objective in Communicating from *telling* to *serving*. What does your staff need from you? What would serving look like? How might you be better able to be the rock to your team by resisting telling, unless it's an "ency" issue – emergency, urgency or proficiency?

Sometimes you get pushback on a "no tell" approach. I was working with a talented group of leaders on a people and culture strategy. Midway through, an e-mail exchange took off like wildfire that the project was confusing and criticism escalated.

A complaint is merely a poorly worded request – a helpful insight. We needed to assist people through the "new" way of self-governed accountability for their growth rather than the typical leadership training sessions of one-way telling. We called an emergency meeting of our core group. We could have defended, reiterated and criticized, and instead, we explored how this initiative was designed to serve them as leaders. A half-hour meeting later, and folks said they left feeling clear, empowered and excited.

Telling or being told may be easier, but it's not transformative.

How do you keep moving the needle as a leader who more often serves versus tells? Rally leaders around you who understand its importance through their actions, who gets things done without relying on imparting, demanding and bombarding?

Have you ever left a boss because you felt, "too listened to and understood?" I doubt it. More likely, you left a role because you felt treated like a number, your ideas weren't welcomed or there was no follow up.

Communication, blissfully, has to happen every minute of every workday and therefore is an opportunity to continually reinforce "you matter here." And people who matter feel like STARs – satisfied, team-oriented, accomplished and ready to stay (retention).

Practice Communication Structures that Work

You know you have delivered information of high quality and relevance in a serving (versus telling) approach when your team can affirmatively make the statements below.

- I know what is expected of me.
- I feel you care about me.
- I know what you need me to do.
- I believe you "get it."

In other words, people have what they need to be FINE.

- Facts – both what is known and what is not known.
- Individualized – it feels like a person, not a robot, is Communicating.
- Next – they know what action to take with this information.
- Empathy – you've put yourself in their shoes.

You can use FINE as a filter for your Communication.

- **F:** Did I include only the relevant facts and in an understandable way?
- **I:** Did it sound like me?
- **N:** Do people know what to do next?
- **E:** Did I make people feel I understood what it must be like for them?

I shared this formula in a *Communication for Clarity and Confidence* micro-learning e-learning course. Hands down, leaders said the FINE formula was the most important tip they took away and applied it immediately.

To break through old habits, push past cultural resistance and attempt new approaches, it's helpful to have formulas to guide us. A formula from my healthcare days that helped improve providers' accuracy, efficiency and relationships is SBAR (Situation, Background, Assessment, Recommendation). Not only does this formula check the Organize box, you can use it to Recognize and promote Kindness too. Check that you've addressed each element in every Communication – verbal and written.

- *Situation:* "Over the last 24 hours …"
- *Background:* "What this means for you is a change in X."
- *Assessment:* "I know this is challenging for Y reasons, and I am so grateful for your Z" (e.g., patience, working extra hours, understanding).
- *Recommendation:* "Here's a tip to …" (make it about them).

You will notice that there was acknowledgment in the first part (under "Situation") showing that you're paying attention. As Theodore Roosevelt said, **"They don't care about what you say until you show you care."** Then, you close with the last part of the formula being all about them too.

The fact that people may be spread across multiple sites, working from home and on-site, that you have growing spans of control (number of direct reports), having consistent formulas for communicating updates, requests and opportunities can save you time, reduce confusion and minimize misunderstanding when what ideally would be shared virtually has to get transmitted in writing.

By the way, having a formula doesn't mean "stiff." Add a dose of "you" to close out your Communication. Love dad jokes? Include one! Into sports? Throw in a sports metaphor. Bigtime complimenter? Add an acknowledgment. Front-ending your communication with a formula like SBAR might, in fact, give you the freedom to close with the personal touch.

Perfect Is the Arch Enemy of Good Communication

Positive perfectionism, or what Brené Brown calls healthy striving,[41] is about trying to ensure you live up to your own standards and do well.

Do you feel added pressure to "make it perfect" because it's in writing and therefore can be misconstrued, or might make it onto social or traditional media? The problem is, this slows things down, reduces our touch points and generally sabotages our good intentions about regular, humanized and practical Communication.

The key is not to get caught up in getting it perfect. More is more. Frequent messaging is ideal. Personalization is more important than perfection. **Human rules over "corporate speak."**

Don't be quiet. If you have something to say, speak up. Make sure you can back it up though.

Stephanie, Talent Acquisitions Professional

TIPS ▸ WHAT WORKS

- Daily updates (posted in shared virtual and physical spaces).
- Video touch points – post a personalized video message as often as you can (can be different platforms for different audiences).
- Use a story to make a point (for a simple story structure, scan the QR Code).
- Use a consistent system for briefings like SBAR.
- When you notice someone's not doing well, check it out (find them coverage if it's serious).
- When a crisis occurs, debrief what happened in real time (bring in experts if necessary).
- Admit when you don't know, something's tough for you and generally be human and "real."

TIPS ▸ WHAT LIKELY DOESN'T WORK

- E-mails to people delivering value and frontline professionals (they are too busy and rarely at a screen to read it and it pulls them away from their value-added work).
- Team meetings that are one-way telling.
- "Just the facts ma'am" – along with facts, acknowledge emotions and frustrations.

- Tell and demand – you may need to be direct in a crisis and clear with non-negotiable expectations, however, don't let it shut down the feedback loop, questions or suggestions.

 Scan the QR Code to access tools to have people give you feedback on how effective your Communication is and to deepen your skills in Communicating effectively during times of crisis and change. You will also find all the footnote content noted in this chapter.

CHAPTER 6

Kindness

"You are too soft."

As my jaw hung open, I couldn't believe what I was hearing. This was the response to a female colleague bringing forward a proposal for an increase in job share positions in the organization. Not, "It's not feasible or it breaks policy." It was, "You are too soft." If there weren't some nods around the table, I might have written it off as a leader who just didn't "get it." Apparently in this case, kindness = pushover.

Sometimes empathy for people is seen as weakness, rather as an important leadership asset.

This leader was, in fact, progressive. She saw before the talent shortage was in full swing that the organization could position themselves as a great place to work by being open to working *with* employees, from a place of understanding and compassion, so they were satisfied and could contribute at a higher level.

As we navigate our way through talent shortages, people increasingly negotiate on the basis of compensation *and* lifestyle, flexibility *and* connectivity, professional growth *and* wellness. Hearing them out isn't just Kind, it's good business sense.

More Than a Business Strategy

We use words like agile, progressive and innovation strategically, however when they don't translate into how we treat our people, they feel the bait and switch. "Wait, you want me to adjust to this change and pick up that responsibility and learn this new thing, yet you're not willing to be understanding and adaptable when I ask you to consider work-life balance needs?" **At the root of adapting and serving employees' needs is Kindness.** Otherwise, those "flexible" strategies can fall right back into the trap of being a corporate "program," policy or budget line that can be cut anytime.

Put another way, flexibility of the organization, and you as leader, communicates that:

- You care about their health,
- You care about their family,
- You want them to pursue their passions and hobbies, and
- You trust they can be productive.

Kindness and empathy can no longer be viewed as "soft" leadership skills. They will be determinants of the employee's relationship with work and a fundamental business imperative.

Cindy, Human Resources Executive

We have to be careful not to fall into the habit of pointing fingers when people resist our corporate structures. To say "those Millennials are entitled" is not only unkind, it also shuts down the opportunity for us to understand what they are looking for in great work. Also be careful as this is dangerously close to ageism; any "ism" is unkind personified!

If employees today want a bigger say in building the job they want, share what Satisfaction means to them and point out what's not working, it might just be in our best interest to listen. Could we partner in an ongoing exploration of "what is possible" together?

Kindness as Currency

As we are seeing the death of the corporate head office, unrelenting demands over people's schedules and command and control leadership, we are seeing what leaders of *all* genders can bring to the table.

Sadly, there is a double-edged sword for those who identify as she/her who were not supported when they needed kindness earlier in their career. One leader shared with me, "It's tough to not get mad sometimes. I needed flexibility as a single mom; I disappointed my kids a lot, came to work sick, was exhausted for years. I support flexible schedules and structures for working parents. I encourage my staff to take advantage of it, but if I'm honest, there's a small part of me that's bothered that this wasn't there for me. Then I see my adult kids more there for their kids, and I remember, I need to show my staff the same compassion."

This self-aware leader knows that the lack of understanding and kindness shown to her cannot be perpetuated. She gets to rewrite the story of her experience by creating the workplace she would have wanted. She can be the leader that she always wanted to work for.

The kind leader. Now that's a legacy.

In any job market, inflexible policies, unsupportive bosses, lack of psychological safety, barriers to advancement and more can deter great people from applying and staying. In our current talent-driven marketplace, kind people, policies and practices are table stakes. For more on this, Roxanne Derhodge substantiates the business value in her book *ROR: Return on Relationships*.

"While AI will hijack the technical and hard-skill elements of leadership, so long as we have humans at work, they will crave the validation, appreciation, and empathy that only humans – not machines – can provide."[42] Kindness is king (ahem, queen) so we best start appreciating this within ourselves and each other, even if not everyone gets it – yet.

Kindness Connects

When I ask successful leaders who identify as she/her mid-career about amazing bosses and mentors, so often I hear that what helped most was this guru sharing a story of how they too had experienced something difficult, painful and perhaps a colossal failure. It's hard to relate to people you put on a pedestal.[43] Sharing failures (small to large) is not only a gesture of Kindness, it also builds trust by demonstrating there's enough psychological safety in the relationship to be vulnerable.

Sometimes as leaders we can't fix an issue, however we can *support* people going through the muck. You have been hardwired to fix the problems people bring to you, taking it on your already ladened leadership shoulders. This can sometimes come from a place of ego, by being the hero, by being indispensable, and by switching to supporter rather than fixer shows your team long-term Kindness.

A Sense of Agency

Being the rock is believing that you have the capacity to find solutions to problems that matter to your team. What if you paused and reflected on how you can help most?

- What is it I know how to do?
- Where is there a need?
- How can I help?[44]

This solution-focused approach[45] requires a Kind and understanding partnership. Even if you, as the leader, can fix it or have an idea of how, it's about holding back on removing the agency of that individual being able to find the solution (possibly not as efficiently, consistently or fully as your solution). This is something you need to be particularly aware of when you have been in their role and have the technical expertise to do the job.

I fall into this trap from time to time as a coach. I want to say, "Oh yes, I've run into that problem! I have three things you should do."

There's a reason coaching schools ingrain that coaches are not to solve problems for people. The majority of a coaching conversation in an exploratory and inquiry phase. The answer is within them. It is with permission that you offer a suggestion.

It may be tough as a coach, and it's ten times tougher for leaders as you have a vested interest in the very problem they've brought to you. However, which will lead to a greater likelihood of action and encourage future self-directed behavior – you telling them what to do or them coming up with their own next step?[46]

When you have faith they have the answer within and you are there to remove barriers, offer assistance and support from the sidelines, you will no doubt be the person that people talk about in the future as one of those influential people they will always remember and be grateful for. Way to go best boss ever in the making!

Kindness Is Easy

We've been talking about some mindset and behavioral steps to lead with Kindness. Ironically, as nebulous as this seems, it's actually quite easy to see in action. And because of that, it's easy to encourage from within the team and role model it.

Kindness looks like any of these scenarios.

- Smiling and saying thank you.
- Showing up in person.
- Saying, "I remember what that was like."
- Admitting it's not easy.

- Expressing gratitude for patience, hard work and even "showing up."
- Pointing out something that's working.
- Reminding what help is available.
- Assuming an issue is a process and not a people problem.

Where appreciation flows, Kindness goes.

As much as we've talked so far about how Kindness shows up in conversations, I'd suggest more often it's what people *don't* see that shows your Kindness.

- Adding extra staff to match workload surges says, "I've got your back."
- Redeploying when roles become redundant says, "Everyone here has a role."
- Asking for ideas says, "Your voice matters."
- Listening to someone in struggle says, "What you're going through matters to me."
- Putting extra debriefing, EAPs[47] and educational resources in place says, "Your well-being matters."
- Not sending an e-mail after hours says, "You deserve your off time."
- Sharing a resource says, "I see your potential."
- Listening to ideas says, "Your opinions are as valuable as mine."
- Hosting team celebrations says, "We are doing amazing things here!"

So much of what you do no one may see, however, it is likely noticed on an intuitive level. Regardless, see your invisible leadership as a gift to yourself. It gives *you* STAR results – greater Satisfaction, a sense of being part of a Team, a sense of Accomplishment, and your Retention.

Kindness Is Self-Care

"Wellness" has become a bit in fashion, and anytime something becomes a trend, cynicism can set in. If it's a corporate program that's not offered in a way that aligns with what people want, can practice or does not address root issues with wellbeing, it can begin to feel like corporate speak. For example, if the company begins offering yoga at lunchtime at head office on Tuesdays, that's lovely but it leaves out people who cannot get away for an hour or work remotely. If the people who need it most cannot access it and wouldn't benefit much beyond a surface level even if they could, it's not a wellness program.

That's where you come in as a rockstar leader.

You can remind people to take their breaks, take deep breaths when they're experiencing heightened arousal and put regular one-on-one (or small group) check-ins on the calendar. For in-person teams, set up a TV to play YouTube videos of yoga versus the news.[48] For remote teams, create a wellness break challenge where everyone posts the self-care activity they did during a half hour of blocked time (walked the dog, ate a scrumptious salad, took a few Duolingo lessons).

Given that 80% of the fibers of the vagus nerve run from the body into the brain, when you remind your staff to engage in wellness and compassionate self-care practices, it can help dial down their arousal system. Role model and share how using breath, movement, play, helpful mantras and smiling are helping you through this challenging time. And if you're not doing it – start. **Your self-Kindness practices help others to practice them too.**

Encourage people to share examples of Kindness they're seeing others perform. Kindness expert Laurie Flasko issues a challenge to do 1,000 random acts of Kindness. Ideally, something like this is in place before a crisis or change initiative launches.

I know you're busy, but there is good news. You and others are already doing Kind things. The more you can point them out, encourage people to notice them and have a way to capture them, the more likely people will see, continue and experience them.

TIPS ▶ WHAT WORKS

- Have a place for people to share Kindness, such as a Kindness board (virtual and physical).
- Include specific examples of Kindness in your communications.
- Invite people to submit Kindness examples through an e-mail (e.g., kindness@companyname.com) or a hashtag (e.g., #kind*companyname*).
- Make Kindness easy by having things like gift cards and compliment cards handy for people to give to each other.
- Start huddles and meetings with someone sharing an act of Kindness they witnessed, did or heard about.

- Notice and acknowledge Kind acts when you see or hear of them.
- Gently remind everyone of calming techniques.
- Create more calming spaces, such as break rooms that have reduced stimuli, calming content on TV screens and messages of appreciation.
- Remind people to turn off work in their evenings, when not on shift and during vacation

TIPS **WHAT LIKELY DOESN'T WORK**

- Challenge people to engage in a certain number of Kind acts when they already feel overwhelmed.
- Make Kindness a mandatory corporate activity during a crisis.
- Take Kindness from the community in ways that are counter-policy (e.g., donated baked goods have to be in the staff room so people can wash their hands).
- Expect everyone to feel comfortable with it (or be on board right away).
- Shame people who are too overwhelmed, compassion-fatigued or burnt out to participate.

For Laurie Flasko's challenge and other magnificent resources to aid you in being a ROCKSTAR leader, scan the QR Code. You will also find all the content for the references noted in this chapter.

CHAPTER 7

What Gets in the Way?

Hopefully by now, some or all of this makes sense. You may also be thinking about all the barriers to making some of this happen.

There are many obstacles that stand in the way of ROCK leadership practices in a crisis or major change. Let's talk about how to be the rock to others *despite* the obstacles.

Hierarchy

Speak up clearly and confidently. Learn to handle anything that may get thrown at you with class.

Star, Professional Coach

An "Executive Sponsor" during change projects can break down barriers, however, there's an undertone of power in this position. If you're running into problems, someone can weigh in and make things happen. That can be helpful in stressful times, but would "Executive Mentor" lend a different tone, yet still have the same gains?

When hierarchy blends with bureaucracy, it stands squarely in the way of ROCK leadership practices. It can sometimes be hard to see if it's in your organization's culture or commonplace in your industry. Here are some signs you have a bureaucratic hierarchy.

- You need two sign-offs to give a $25 gift card.
- A good idea needs to go through a committee before it's trialed.
- Budgets are built in an office and "told" to the people responsible for them.

- Leaders have not been to the front line during a crisis or change yet call all the shots from the boardroom.
- Staff can't tell you the names of their leaders.

This unhelpful kind of hierarchy stifles innovation, volunteerism and connection. It can create competitiveness, silos and hoarding of information. It may seem like favoritism is present, reduces the likelihood those "at the top" will be informed of what's "really" happening and rewards those who play the political game well. Those who identify as she/her, including leaders, believe they will get noticed through hard work, but that is a mismatch with hierarchy because they're not "playing the game."[49]

Lack of Accountability

If you were to ask anyone in your organization if it is important to be responsible, the odds are they would say, "Of course!" **Taking responsibility is a key element in being accountable** – to each other, to quality work, to meeting deadlines, to moving in the same direction toward the same goals – and yet lack of accountability is shared as a pressing issue by so many clients.

The Ladder of Accountability[50] is a powerful tool that will help you understand that people are somewhere on their journey to becoming more accountable; it's not binary. It will assist you in noticing signs of progress, and how to help it along when it's slow (check out our version at greatnessmagnified.com/rockstar).

Climate describes the shared perceptions of the people in a group or organization, while culture includes how people feel about the organization and the beliefs, values and assumptions that provide the identity and set the standards of behavior.[51] Does the climate of your workplace reinforce and enable lack of accountability? You're the rock to your staff if you work to address this, rather than point the blame at them.

Rockstar leaders find that most people are willing to be more accountable, as long as they know what's expected, have the resources to be successful and are supported to persevere and find solutions when inevitable barriers arise.

Generally, promotions are awarded because someone is good technically, yet sometimes the tools to adjust, develop and evolve are not provided, especially in new management roles.[52] This is happening at an accelerated pace in response to the talent shortages of today, particularly in frontline human services fields largely dominated by those who identify as she/her.

Ensure people *can* take responsibility for what they have control over, they have access to training to close skill gaps, know what is expected of them, are in an environment free of shame and blame and they have a way of surfacing and solution-finding their way through barriers to performance.

Uncertainty

Did you know that doctors working in a hospital are the "most responsible person" for the patient, and yet have no control over the staff ratio, who is hired or how the team is trained? Furthermore, hospitals in Canada don't know their full funding formula until after the fiscal year has begun, yet must make operational and strategic decisions based on working assumptions. Uncertainty, and angst related to it, is the day-to-day reality of frontline providers, leaders and policy makers. Now, think about the trickle-down impact that has on the patient. Yikes!

Healthcare is not the only sector plagued with uncertainty. It may simply take different forms.

We often talk about resistance to change and that "change is hard." **What if it's not the change itself as much as the uncertainty that coincides with it?**

Leaders that are the rock to their stars acknowledge the signs of strain caused by uncertainty. You've had times, personally and professionally, where things just become "too much." Uncertainty can be reduced by aligning strengths to what needs to get done (Recognition), streamlining priorities (Organization), clarifying what is happening and why it's important (Communication) and expressing a belief that individually and collectively "you've got this" (Kindness).

Through truly listening to the uncertainty, you build psychological safety. I continually remind rockstar leaders, **"If people are complaining to you, that means they trust you!"** Talk about a mental reshuffle. You mean that negativity is a good thing? Yes, as I shared earlier, a complaint is merely a poorly worded request. "I don't know if I can handle this" might come across as "we've always done it this way," "it won't work" or "we can't handle one more thing." What if you expected this, and knew the reaction to change was "right on schedule." It's not a problem to solve as a leader. It's simply a byproduct of uncertainty.

Empathize through the struggle and together you will find a way through with greater clarity and connection.

Overload

Workload is like a leaky faucet – drip, drip, drip. One more e-mail, one more project, one more report. It adds up until the sink overflows (you cancel your vacation, you miss your deadline, you dread Monday mornings). It all adds up to tsunami-like strain, and, somehow, you need to reach in and pull the plug to let some of that water out.

Here's a few guiding principles that can help you make decisions and take action, even when you feel overwhelmed.

* If it's not a heck yes, it's a no.
* If it has to be done more than once, create a process.
* If it's non-negotiable, put a cap on the time allotted and work within that constraint.

The more you practice these and other "anti-overwhelm" strategies, the less your overload is, and the more you advocate for making work more manageable for staff too. If you believe "nothing can be done," then how likely are you to advocate, explore solutions and experiment with lowering-the-load approaches?

If everything's important, then nothing's important. In overload, it's essential to stay grounded in reality and co-create solutions. You can ask yourself or your team these REAL questions.

> *All your thinking cells are not in your brain. The enteric nervous system contains over 100 million nerve cells lining your gastrointestinal tract. Trust your gut feeling.*
>
> Nathalie, Coach & Speaker

* R – What is the *real* (root) issue?
* E – What is a realistic *expectation*?
* A – What is the easiest *action* we can take to start to address the issue?
* L – What do we hope to *learn* from this next action?

It may seem counterintuitive to put pressure on your time, ways of working and processes when feeling overwhelmed. However, together, you might address the overload issues in the longer term and what is truly driving it.

Also, consider putting some time limits on fixes. Parkinson's Law proposes that time expands to the time we give it. Force a first-next-steps approach and leave the rest.

If you're overwhelmed, chances are that's true of your staff too. Reducing the burden is necessary for STAR results, for you and your team to be Satisfied, work well as a Team, feel a sense of Accomplishment, and refrain from looking elsewhere in order to Retain all of your rockstars. Make work overload a team goal to address.

In other words, make your team mantra, "If I can't remember it next year, how important is it today?"

By the way, if you feel really uncomfortable pushing back, challenging and even advocating for this, think about what is suffering as a result of you feeling overwhelmed? Does your partner feel second fiddle to your work, have you given up the gym, have you lost touch with friends?

Silos

Many organizations have inadvertently built divisions that disconnect. Pointing to "working remotely" as being the reason for disconnection minimizes the fact that divisions existed before.

Work structure is rarely the *root* problem. If recent changes were the first time it felt like some departments had priority over others, some voices counted more than others and resources were inequitably allocated, then sure, that is likely to be a problem. However, more likely there are invisible silos that reinforce an "us and them" approach that may inadvertently become embedded into leadership behaviors and attitudes.

To be the rock to others, they need to feel you "get" them, you care about them, you're invested in them. This is true of your staff, departments, customers, even your boss!

Where you really see silos is when there's a major change, crisis or upheaval. To counteract this, leaders, you may be forced outside of your comfort zone to lend a hand. Solutions to inevitable issues are more likely to be found *with* groups coming together, and, in fact, can be the perfect opportunity to "desilo." It's where it can become clear just how interdependent departments and individuals are. **You can turn toward or turn against; one gets results, the other disrupts.**

Studies of the leadership style of those who identify as she/her reveal evidence of nurturing, inclusiveness and collaborative strategies, encouraging participation. In times of change, we can lean on the skills and experiences already present.[53]

This is also a time to notice what people are great at to make changes that may transcend the crisis at hand. Could someone be identified as an emerging leader? Might this be the perfect opportunity to re-engage someone through redeployment? How might cross-functional teams be able to continue with a new mandate?

People may not like getting out of their silos, including leaders, however silos are already having a largely invisible negative impact. Change is the ideal opportunity to test the boundaries of them and perhaps crack them open.

Incivility and Lack of Psychological Safety

During COVID,[54] many were laid off and furloughed. What shocked most is when employees didn't choose to return; the quit rate stayed high.[55]

We cannot blame it all on COVID. There was a movement afoot with people opting out of workplaces that were counter to health, well-being and satisfaction. It simply wasn't large enough for the public-at-large to notice. In many media interviews I've been asked, "Why is this happening now?" It's not just now; it's just now it's hitting the bottom line, disrupting business and creating operational chaos.

When people have options, they go where they are valued and respected.

How this relates directly back to psychological safety is that choice – of industry, company, job and even boss – enables employees to *deselect* what doesn't meet their expectations of safe, respectful and stimulating work. You've had enough experience with toxic work environments to know the signs, and people are willing to leave versus tough it out because they can.

Over coffee with friends, in the staff room, at association meetings, at the dinner table, we've been reflecting.

* What do I want?
* What do I need?
* What am I not willing to tolerate?
* What gives meaning and spirit to me?
* What changes do I need to make?

To get STAR results, people need to feel psychologically safe – to share their ideas, to stand up to bullies, to report unsafe work, to make suggestions for improvement, to express feelings, to discuss failures, to be themselves. And the good news? Everything on this list that employees, and leaders alike, want is also what the organization wants. It's a win-win when psychological safety is present and preserved with unwavering commitment.

Even in the midst of chaos, you can set the tone for long-term healthier habits, cultural philosophies and leadership practices. **This, my ROCKSTAR friends, is how you build a legacy.**

 Scan the QR Code to get lots of great resources to aid you in being a ROCKSTAR leader, including our version of the Accountability Ladder. You will also find all the content for the references noted in this chapter.

CHAPTER 8

Aim for STAR Results

I have a theory. Many of the things we intuitively knew we should do as kids to build connections – thank someone, say please, smile, share, show kindness when someone is struggling – are undervalued as professionals.

These skills don't let you stand apart from the rest and nowhere is "smiling" an endorsable skill on LinkedIn. There is no national knowledge exam or college entrance test that requires these abilities. It's not an explicitly stated prerequisite on professional-level job postings. And yet, research shows that relationship-building behaviors and having strong emotional intelligence will be a difference-maker in your career. [56] [57] [58]

In times of stress and strain, never are these basic humanizing gestures more needed from you as a leader. Simple things that remind staff they are stars in your eyes. These simple gestures communicate implicitly:

* I see you,
* I care about you and
* I value you.

From ROCK to STAR

So far in *ROCKSTAR*, I've shared the four essential ingredients to lead through crisis and change. In this chapter, I'm going to give you the evidence of the ROE – return on energy – of ROCK leadership practices. With over 20 years of experience in organizational development, coaching hundreds of leaders, writing hundreds of articles[59] and five books later, I want to share with you the evidence of why your ROCK leadership practices will pay back in STAR dividends.

And what are those dividends? Your team will have a sense of Satisfaction, they'll work together as a Team to achieve shared outcomes, they'll Accomplish key daily tasks as well as special projects and you'll Retain them – they'll stay and you'll likely attract other top talent like them.

It's a win-win all around. Staff are more fulfilled and devoted; as a leader your work becomes more about achievement and execution and less about putting out fires; boards of directors, leaders and owners are happier because strategic priorities are completed and engagement survey scores are up; customers are more satisfied and get better service; your public reputation is better from informal reviews to perhaps being spotlighted as industry leaders.

Crises and major upheavals – externally driven or internally planned – are resource-intensive, sometimes exhausting and often all-consuming. The transformational changes represent a small percentage of your working life, yet likely take up a greater proportion of your memory bank allocated for "work."[60] When that memory is negative, the detail of that memory is even stronger.[61] Practicing ROCK leadership *during* change not only reduces strain in the short term, it creates more positive beliefs about work afterward.

Your brain might actually like change, if you give it a chance to experience STAR benefits.

Satisfaction

In having led or overseen more than one hundred team consultations, I know one thing for certain: **It's not the way through the change that is the hardest, it's *right after* the first signs of getting to "this is the way things are now."**

Why is this? Shouldn't people be more Satisfied and feel good? We got through it! We can put this behind us! Look at what we Accomplished! It was awesome how well we pulled together!

Here's the reality. Most of us experience some degree of burn out. All the little acts of incivility or perceptions of unfairness or beliefs that "I worked harder than you did" finally have time to surface. The decrease in and lack of communication leaves unanswered questions hanging and offers space for rumors to blossom. We saw this post COVID, and you have seen this on a smaller scale at other times in your career, guaranteed.

Don't get me wrong, I'm not saying people are deliberately trying to be problematic. It's just that the pressure valve has to be released. You now have a slow leak of negativity seeping into the air, making it harder to breathe and making you, inadvertently, want to stay away. Who could blame you? You're tired too.

In the absence of sustained ROCK leadership, a haze of dissatisfaction sets in.[62]

It's not just the staff or leader who had to get through this difficult time. It's their families and the other people in their lives. If they came home snappy, were away from their loved ones more or not able to "pull their weight," chances are they've been getting some flack about it. (You might relate to this personally too.)

Family and partners can get behind your staff for a period of time when the push is on, providing support, picking up the slack and telling themselves the change will last only so long, but patience wears thin when the family has been holding on until "this is over" (as if there is a definitive end point) in order to cope. They want their loved one "back" – physically, mentally, emotionally, socially. If staff are burnt out, change fatigued and unable to find a functional work rhythm, it's hard for people outside the system to continually understand and sympathize with "whatever is going on at your workplace."

The pride of sharing the news as the change leader and "my wife is a superstar" can become "my wife is a martyr" virtually overnight. Kids say, "Can you play with me *now*?" and mom/aunt/grandma guilt enters the scene.

Set staff up for success by digging into how your ROCK leadership can build Satisfaction to keep them resourceful and resilient personally and professionally.

Individuals and teams that are recognized are significantly more engaged and Satisfied.[63] [64] This statistic is true during times of stability, so it stands to reason that the more appreciated and valued people are when they are under extreme strain, the more likely they are to respond positively to survey statements such as, "I feel that my ideas are listened to" or "in the last month I was told how my work made a contribution" or "my direct supervisor has given me feedback this month."

Ask questions. Wait until you are satisfied with the answer.

Haley, Manager

I've seen this in action. When leaders managing teams with high dissatisfaction and low engagement are shown how to recognize people consistently and effectively every day, they report an immediate improvement in staff's willingness to collaborate, communicate and innovate, which brings us to the next aspect of STAR.

Teamwork

When individuals are treated like a number and do not feel their efforts are uniquely valued, they can still manage to come in and work flat out through a time-bound change or crisis. Often there is so much to do and everyone does the best they can, jumping in where necessary. As best as possible, a plan for the day is often formed, however the reality of crisis mode is that individuals do as much as physically possible and within their control to meet the immediate needs right in front of them. And those needs can change in the space of minutes.

Often, if an individual notices a colleague is overwhelmed and floundering, they'll pitch in. Old wrongs are put aside for the good of customers. Everyone is needed. All hands are on deck.

When leaders are the rocks to their staff, they help keep that Teamwork going. They notice examples of it and say, "Thanks for helping Sam out in addressing our backlog." They say to Sam, "Thanks for letting Kabir lend a hand. That was really collaborative of you." They find ways to share multiple examples in all-staff communications – a video, weekly briefing, social media post – fueling pride and a sense that we're all in this together.

In other words, ROCK leaders provide regular updates so people can see what's happening all around them and feel a sense of "us." When staff are head down, getting done what is in front of them, as a leader, you can ensure each individual feels a part of a larger whole. People need to know the big picture, and you can provide it for them, so they can get their head back down and keep going.

Similarly, after a major change, ROCK leadership helps Teams celebrate how well they pulled together, deconstruct what worked, discuss how that can be replicated and standardized going forward. They find ways to keep encouraging and recognizing small and larger gestures of continued Team-first behaviors.

Accomplishment

In the midst of crisis and change, there is too much to do. On the one hand, times of upheaval can give us the yummy neurological release of dopamine when we Accomplish tasks, take action and fix immediate problems.

But, let's get real for a moment. For this to feel like a sense of achievement, we need to have enough time to realize the Accomplishment and have shared value for it, not minimize its importance and bury it in the litany of tasks that we don't get time to do.

In times of crisis and change, all too often this recipe for that dopamine hit evades you and your staff. Also, you can get addicted to the "quick fix" rush that perpetuates the "leader solves the problems" cycle that inadvertently disempowers staff, reinforces "us and them" silos and keeps you run off your feet and in the weeds of management.

As a leader, your ROCK behaviors allow people to be empowered to find solutions and digest the sense of Accomplishment from progress made. Your empathy and compassion allow you to say things like, "Try it and report back" and "What ideas do you have" and "You're doing the best you can and that's exactly what we expect of you." Many professionals come to work every day feeling already behind the eight ball – unanswered e-mails, too full schedules, overwhelming workloads, increasing expectations by customers.

Those who identify as she/her in STEM (science, technology, engineering, math) and other industries dominated by those who define themselves as he/him need to be very mindful of this.[65] A lack of role models and someone to "catch" you when you're beating yourself up requires some vigilance on your part. Experts like Emily Nichols are helping to change this. In the meantime, catch yourself when you're counting all the ways you're *not* Accomplishing goals versus how many you are.

I remember reading a story about New York doctors interviewed about their take on the COVID crisis at the beginning of the pandemic. "We are not at all in control of this and it's going to get worse before it gets better." Most of the world was probably freaked out. What I saw in these doctors, at the front line of health history, the epicenter of the first wave of the COVID-19 outbreak in the US, were people who were saying they were letting people down.[66] This quote is the evidence for why we need to remind high performers doing their best that they are stars as they may not see it in themselves, including when they need to most.

As the expression goes, **the person who feels appreciated will always do more than is expected.**[67] Help people to appreciate their own Accomplishments so they are achievement motivated versus (in)adequacy demotivated.

As a leader, you will try to unblock specific barriers to Achievement – advocate for another position, lend a hand, source more supplies, facilitate a conversation. What is within your control is your ability to make people believe that they have achieved and Accomplished important work *despite* all of the barriers. The ripple effect is that all of these ideas and more fuels the Team motivation and Satisfaction, further reinforcing the S and T of STAR.

Ironically, by doing this for others, you will also notice more of your Accomplishments. How about you ask yourself every day:

* What can I acknowledge I got done today?
* How have I helped others realize how much they achieved today?
* How did I help people reframe what they did versus didn't get done today?

When you can safely answer all of these questions with satisfaction, you too will feel the sense of Accomplishment you deserve to experience during change and challenging times.

Retention

It's been said that, "People don't leave organizations, they leave bosses." Unfortunately, it's not just coffee table wisdom; it remains at or near the top of reasons why people leave.[68] [69] [70] ROCK behaviors change that.

People who feel valued are more likely to stay. The best predictor of Retention is that people are highly Satisfied with Recognition by their boss and peers.[71] [72]

We have spoken a great deal so far about the challenges of Retention in today's job market, and, as negative as it seems, this is actually really good news for you: **people want to work for you. They're looking for you!** They are auditioning bosses and their organizations at increasing rates, and they're happy to keep moving until they find you.

When you lead with ROCK behaviors, you attract others' talent if they are dissatisfied and feel unappreciated. You will also keep them longer than your competitors too.

The clearer individuals are on what is expected of them, what the priorities are and who they can rely on within the team, the more productive, greater sense of Accomplishment and higher quality outcomes they will have.

Although it's virtually impossible to get to all the things they want to in a workday under normal circumstances, let alone during a crisis or a major change, taking unnecessary work off their plates, streamlining systems and listening to feedback about what needs to be addressed goes a long way to ensure people leave their day feeling a sense of Accomplishment and confidence they did their best by their customers and colleagues.

If people feel out of the loop, confused or unsure what is expected of them, it stands to reason that people will look for somewhere Communication is better – and the data shows this.[73][74][75] People who feel leaders are doing their best to Communicate are more likely to meet expectations – of peers and customers – and have less role confusion so they can be productive. (There's less gossip and spreading of rumors if you're Satisfied and clear what's expected of you!)

It is actually psychologically uncomfortable to treat someone poorly when they've been Kind to you. The theory of reciprocity says that when something generous is done to you, you feel a sense of discomfort until you return the favor.[76] Remember, people may forget what you do or say, but they don't forget how you make them feel. **Role model Kindness, and staff will be more likely to follow your lead with their peers and customers (and you).** Make it easy for people to be Kind and reinforce that you're seeing Kindness or gestures of Kindness staff may not be aware of.

Women often are the best caregivers to others but fail to meet their own needs. Self-love and self-compassion are the greatest gifts you will ever give yourself.

Mastora, Therapist

You want people to say on the other side of a crisis or change, "If we can survive this, we can survive anything together." Your staff are smart people. They see the grass isn't necessarily greener on the other side; they know other organizations are going through crises and change right along with them. Use the current situation to remind people why they belong to your organization; don't leave any doubt in their minds that they're in the right place.

Scan this QR Code to get lots of great resources to aid you in being the ROCKSTAR leader you and your employees deserve. You will also find all the content for the references noted in each chapter.

ROCKing the
Future of Work

Picture this.

You have just been handed a fresh sheet of paper and a really nice pen. (Yes, techie friends, you can swap out for a tablet and fancy stylus if you prefer.) Your task is to create the job you want.

You get to start from scratch, pulling the best of what is. You get to decide what strengths and skills you will use every day. You are able to outline your perfect day, what responsibilities you fulfill and how your work structure will enable you to perform at your best.

Don't forget the "build your boss" part! Outline how your boss will communicate with you, lend support, allocate work and set expectations.

And the best part, you are allowed to use all of the things you know now, and only the lessons – not the pain – from any traumatizing experiences, toxic people or crushing experiences.

Perhaps you're actually going to put the book down and do this? Go for it!

What did you notice? What would your ideal work, colleagues and boss look like?

Whether you literally did it or you just had a few aha moments simply by reading the description, you no doubt have some clarity of what you most want and need. **In effect, you have designed your own version of ROCKSTAR.**

- How you want to be Recognized and have good work reinforced.
- How you need work to be Organized so you feel capable and competent.

- How Communication should flow for productivity and connectivity.
- How Kindness is shown by you and others.
- What Satisfaction looks and feels like to you.
- What Teamwork behaviors must be present to perform well.
- What a sense of Accomplishment feels like for you and the work associated with it.
- What it would take to Retain you as the loyal, effective and engaged rockstar you are.

What if you could "blank sheet" a successful project, a healthy organizational change, an effective team, a high performing organization? What if you weren't afraid to reveal the things that were needed for you to be the rock to your stars and "course correct" the gaps?

Whether you're forced to (such as from mass turnover, a reputation crisis, unprecedented expansion or unfortunate downsizing) or you choose to create this ideal scenario proactively, **the future of work can be created with intention.**

Change and crises offer the perfect opportunity for such reflection, even if it seems you don't have time, energy or hope that your ideal work is possible. What if someone told you at the very end of your career, "Oh shoot, didn't you realize you could have had way more of what fuels you and a lot less of what didn't!" If you knew that for sure, wouldn't you do something about it today?

Being the rock to others requires you to be the rock to yourself, and that may mean putting your work needs higher on the list. Unless you design, ask and create it, how do you know it's not possible?

Crafting your preferred future through the momentum that transformation creates may be less work than trying to jumpstart it when things are less chaotic. You're already knee-deep in uncertainty and upheaval; why not come out the other side with clarity and momentum to lead the way that brings the most meaning and spirit to you and others?

Facilitated conversations about both the change *and* the gains for individuals in organizations fuels buy-in at a deeper level too. Fellow speaker Tim Arnold calls this "leading with and" in his book of the same name.[77] Why not embrace that competing priorities are a reality of today's complex world of work; in these conversations, seek to understand and capitalize on the best of change

> *Don't focus on why you can't do things. Focus on how you can. Then get going.*
>
> Linda, Business Consultant

and legacy, individual needs *and* team needs, achievement *and* rest.

As Andy Goodman put it, "Numbers numb, jargon jars, and nobody ever marched on Washington because of a pie chart." Make your change human by making it about the very humans that depend on you to be their rock.

We're behind you. Reach out to us at info@greatnessmagnified.com to let us know how we can help and grab all the resources you need, including facilitated conversation outlines by scanning any of the QR Codes throughout the book.

Let's address the pay-equity gaps, work-life imbalance, the unconscious bias and the many additional barriers to the advancement of those who identify as she/her. Let's refocus on satisfaction and success through the forward momentum that change can afford us. Let's ensure we've hardwired ways of working so that people of all genders know they matter, feel a sense of belonging and have equal opportunities to be stars.

It's only a fairytale if we don't believe it could happen.

Afterword

As women, historically the primary caregivers in our society, we are adept at change – our children demand it. This skillset translates well to the workplace. While women are faced with some unique challenges in the workforce, they also bring a different approach and leadership style to the workplace – one that is welcomed with the shifts in today's labor market. Investing in the leadership capacity of the female workforce is paying off in spades for the adopters. But that doesn't mean that it's completely smooth sailing.

As women step into leadership roles, we are often in what is referred to as the "Double Bind." When women lead like men and take charge, they are strong, decisive, and assertive, which others often see as competent, but they are rarely liked. The flip side of this stereotype is when woman lead with care, they are nurturing of their people, considerate of the emotional impacts, and have a demonstrated commitment to communication. Here they are often well-liked but not necessarily seen as competent. How can we create a work environment where we are seen as competent *and* caring? The challenge to buck these long-standing stereotypes is at a pivotal moment in society's development. Today's workforce is demanding more flexibility to meet the multiple demands on their time and they simply are not willing to put this most valuable resource into a workplace that does not care about them as people.

None of this should be news to you, but what do we do about it? Here is what a collective of committed women in northeastern BC did to shift the paradigm.

In the early fall of 2013, a group gathered to discuss the need for professional and leadership development in a rural part of British Columbia. The local economy was growing; the job board had become the job wall. The natural resource sector, primarily the energy sector, was the dominant pillar of the local economy. When we spoke with local employers about their workforce pressures, a theme quickly became apparent. They were able to recruit for the entry-level positions but finding the skilled labor to step up into supervisory and leadership roles was where the real challenge occurred. They were committed to investing in their own people to promote from within, but building the capacity internally required time away from the office – time they could not spare. These professional and leadership development opportunities most often required travel to a major urban center, adding significantly to the cost of investing in their people.

This group of committed professionals from across a variety of sectors, including local government, post-secondary, and the private sector, set to create the capacity-building opportunity that would support the economic growth of the local businesses and organizations while reducing the pressures on the bottom line. With natural resource sectors being the star of the local economy, the decision was made to support women in the region. It was important to recognize the additional pressures for women in the workforce, particularly in these male-dominated fields, and the challenges traveling for work put on homelife. So, the Spark Women's Leadership Conference was born and has been serving the workforce of northeastern BC since 2014.

Spark's goal is to provide a conference with motivational, inspirational, and professional skill development that creates an environment where women can learn, not only from the high-caliber speakers who grace the stage, but their co-workers and fellow attendees. It creates a safe space to talk about the shared and unique challenges the women of the region face. While building capacity with the attendees – people from across all sectors and all stages of their career – was the primary goal at the onset, it quickly became apparent that the connections to this community were the biggest value to the attendees. They now have a network that understands the pressures they are feeling and can offer support and suggestions on how to navigate the obstacles in front of them.

In its ten-year life, Spark has grown the size of the annual conference and worked to offer additional development options through workshops and other learning opportunities year-round. Spark was built on the sweat equity of volunteers who cared about their community and wanted to see it blossom through dedicated care and attention. While we set the stage to build capacity with the attendees, it is important to walk the talk and build capacity within the steering committee. This group of women supports each other through professional aspirations, entrepreneurial goals, and personal endeavors. It pushes the members to try new things and take risks, knowing they will be supported regardless of the outcome. This is the true power of community and is a demonstrated example of Sarah's ROCKSTAR approach.

Our team is small but mighty and each member plays an important role in delivering these important capacity building opportunities to our region.

We are dedicated to Recognizing the work done; we work hard to be Organized (you can't plan a conference for 300 people without a lot of organization); Communication is vital to our success, and we treat each other with Kindness and compassion as we bring our passion project to life each year. The women who serve on the steering committee remain committed to the work we do because we feel Satisfaction with the opportunity to serve the community; we see the power of Teamwork in delivering something exceptional; we revel in the sense of Accomplishment as attendees share their appreciation for the change Spark has brought their professional lives, and the Retention rate is high with an average of six years of service within the current steering committee. Since Spark's inception in 2014 until today in 2023, twenty-three women have sat at the steering committee table and those who have departed, making room for new perspectives at the table, are still avid champions for Spark.

So why is Spark writing the Afterword to ROCKSTAR – *Magnifying Your Greatness in Times of Change*? The answer is simple. Sarah's work aligns with the work we are doing each and every day. The principles of ROCK Behaviors and STAR Outcomes are exactly the capacity we are supporting through the development of our annual conference and other initiatives. We know this work requires constant attention as the playing field is constantly shifting and evolving, and we must have the skills to understand and adapt to the environment around us.

The pandemic certainly highlighted and accelerated many challenges in the workplace, but they were already happening before the world had a sudden and severe shift. We learned a lot about ourselves and our teams during this historical time in our evolution. We learned about the vital importance of taking care of our people. We continue to learn what is working and isn't. When one of our founding steering committee members was a young girl, her father shared this wise insight with his daughter:

"If we take care of our people, they will take care of our business."

After all, if we don't have people, then we don't have the businesses and organizations that are fundamental to our society. These ROCKSTAR principles are foundational to building a culture in your organization that will reap the benefits of committed, passionate people who will advance your mission and improve your bottom line.

The Woman of Spark

About Sarah

Sarah helps organizations leverage the exponential power of recognition to retain top talent and delight customers. She has a BA (Psych), MSc (Family Relations) and certifications in Human Resources, Organizational Development, Healthcare Administration, and Coaching. She is also one of only 700 with the earned CSP – Certified Speaking Professional – designation. Sarah left a hospital senior leadership role ten years ago to launch Greatness Magnified when one of her kids had a serious mental health crisis. Her child now fully recovered (and both thriving), she speaks internationally, coaches leaders, writes, and (when no one is looking) hip hop dances.

WAYS TO KEEP IN TOUCH WITH SARAH!

Facebook	Sarah McVanel Greatness Magnified	@SarahMcVanel @greatnessmagnif
Instagram	Sarah McVanel Greatness Magnified	@SarahMcVanel @GreatnessMagnified
LinkedIn	Sarah McVanel	linkedin.com/in/sarahmcvanel/ linkedin.com/company/greatnessmagnified/
YouTube	Sarah McVanel	youtube.com/c/SarahMcVanel
Goodreads	Sarah McVanel Author	goodreads.com/author/show/14767373.Sarah_McVanel

How Sarah Can Help You and Your Organization

1. **Valuable Resources** – Visit greatnessmagnified.com/coolstuff/ to download a litany of useful tools, exercises and infographics for immediate success

2. **Request a Strategy Session** – Want specific ideas about how to scale and spread the strategies in this book? Book a strategy session with us by e-mailing info@greatnessmagnified.com

3. **Book Sarah to Speak** – Want Sarah to motivate your team, organization or association into action? For keynote and training topics and to learn about our 100% in, above and beyond client-first approach, visit Sarah at greatnessmagnified.com/speaking

4. **Coach with Greatness Magnified** – Ready to level up your ROCK leadership? Work with Sarah and her team of dynamic coaches. E-mail info@greatnessmagnified.com

**Find all Sarah's books on GoodReads or
visit greatnessmagnified.com/store**

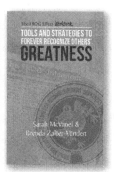